Haiku Day

Poems from: Issa,   Basho,   Buson,   Gansan,   Chori

Illustrations by chud fmalt

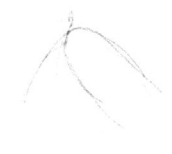

The illustrations in this book were done in oil paint on board and paper.
For more visit: www.sky-in-session.com

Copyright © 2014 Chad Smalt
All rights reserved.
ISBN-13: 978-1502372451
ISBN-10: 1502372452

Starting on a Spring morning

these 12 Haiku's and 12 paintings

illustrate the passing of each season

ending in a winter night.

The world of dew
is the world of dew
and yet, and yet -

-Issa

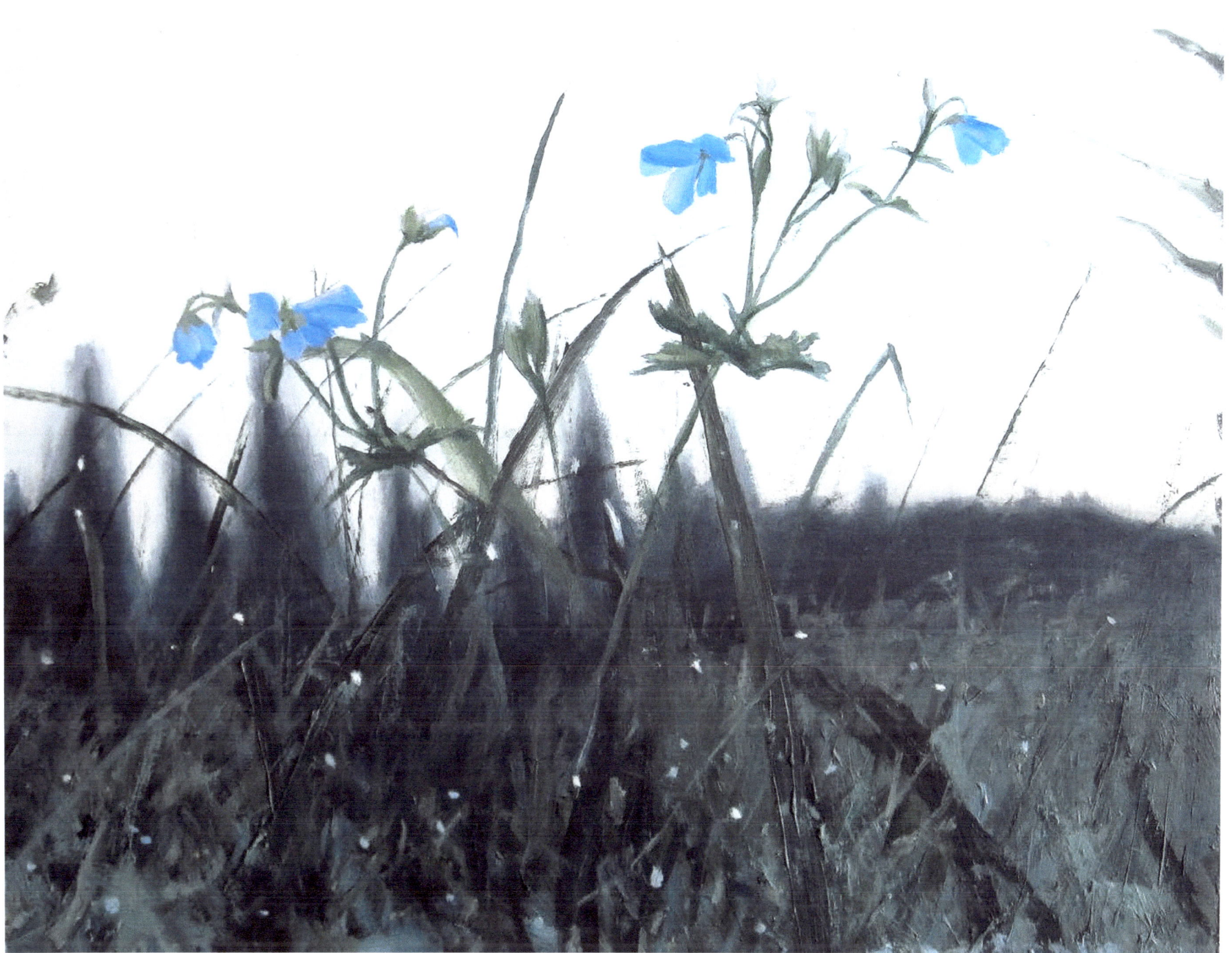

Spring!
a nameless hill
in the haze

-Basho

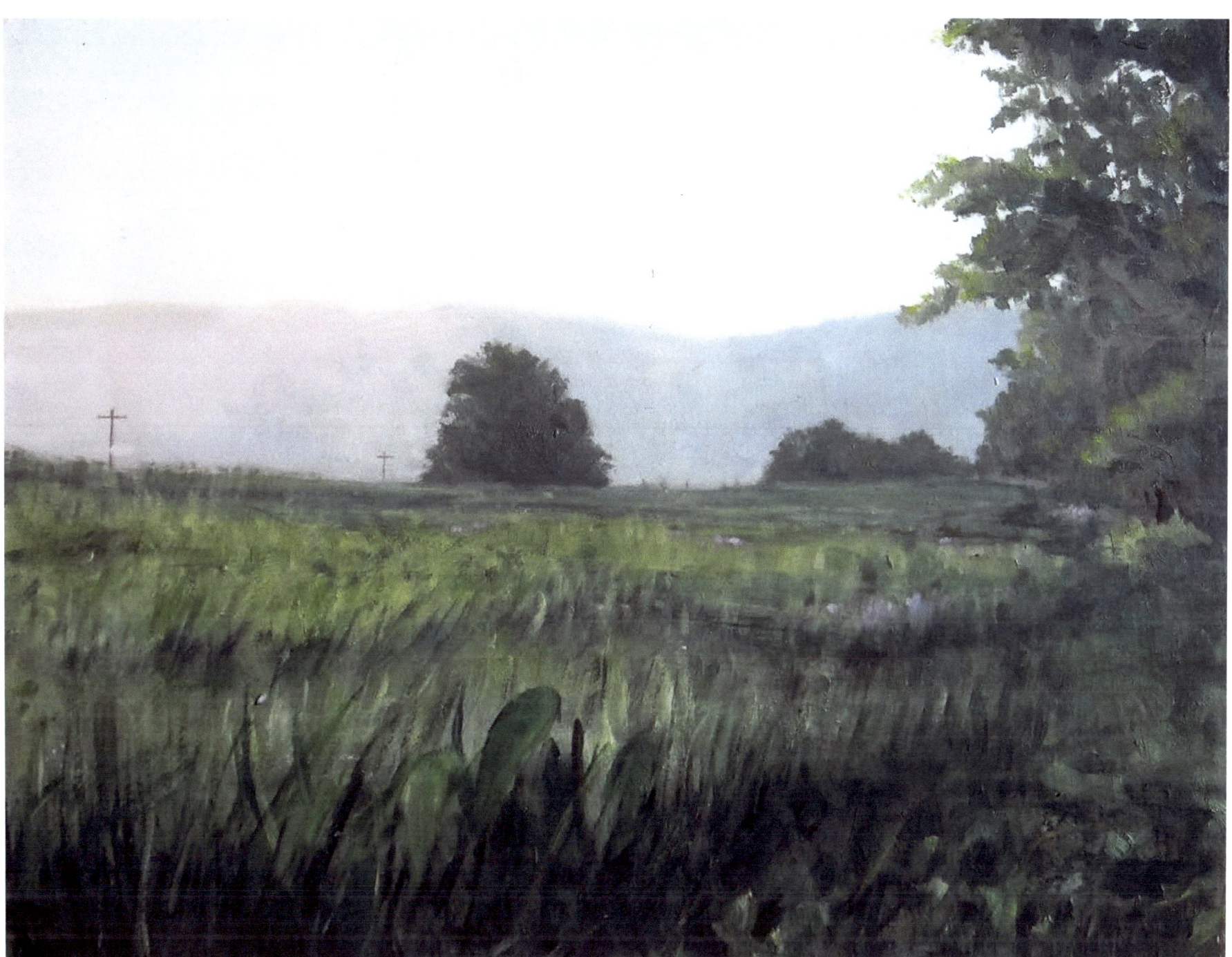

Coming back
so many pathways
through the spring grass.

- Buson

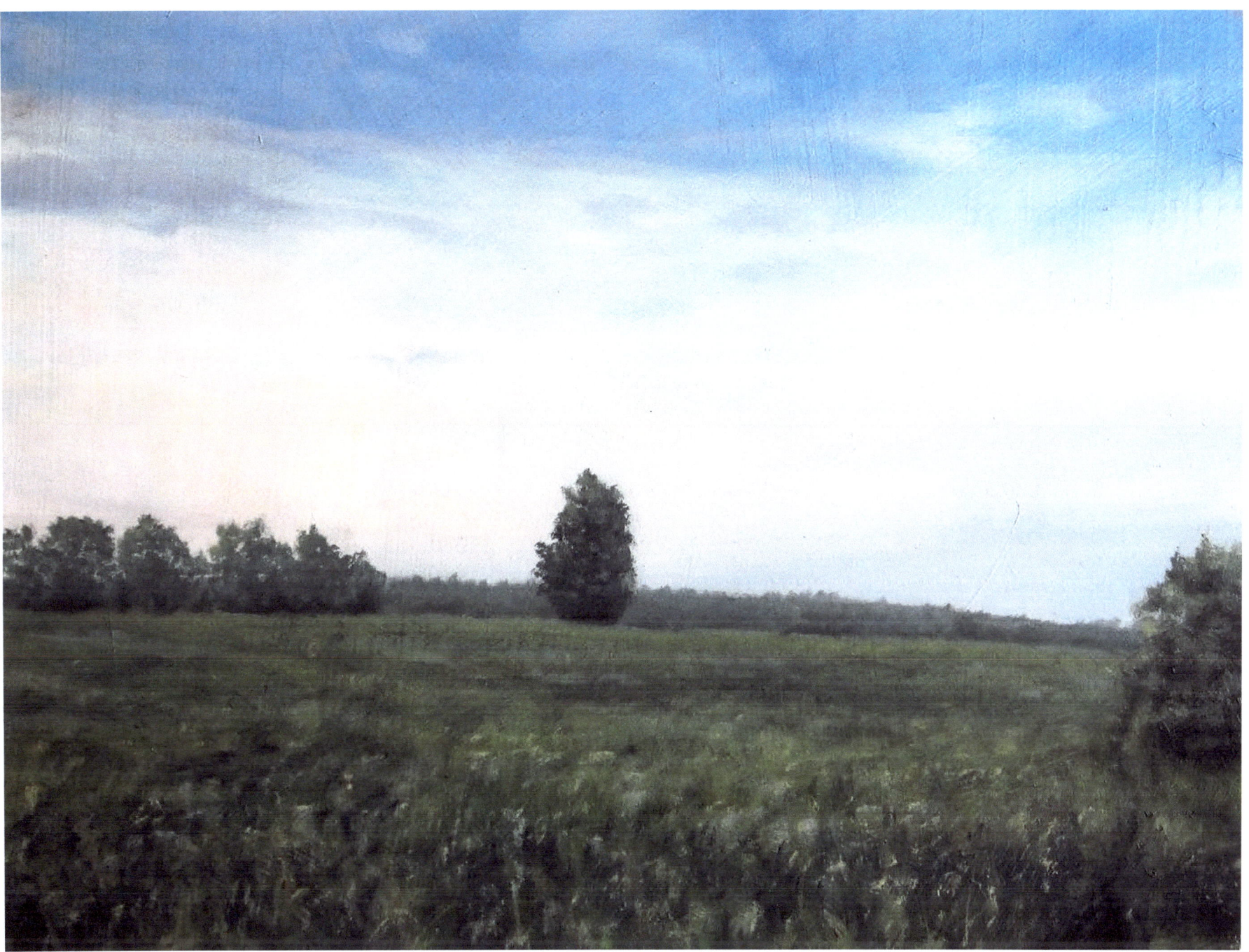

Early summer rain
houses facing the river
two of them.

-Buson

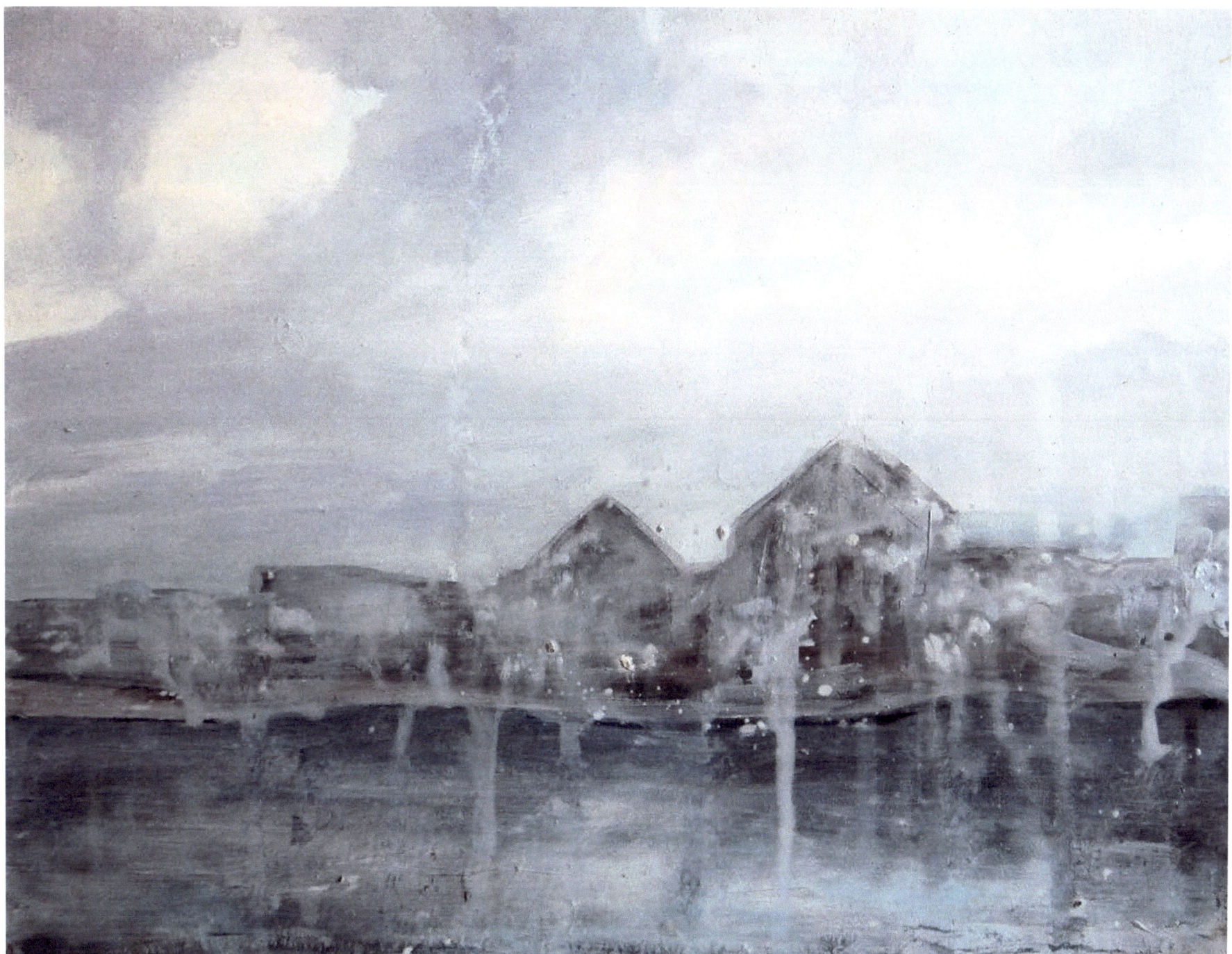

A petal shower
of mountain roses
and the sound of rapids.

-Basho

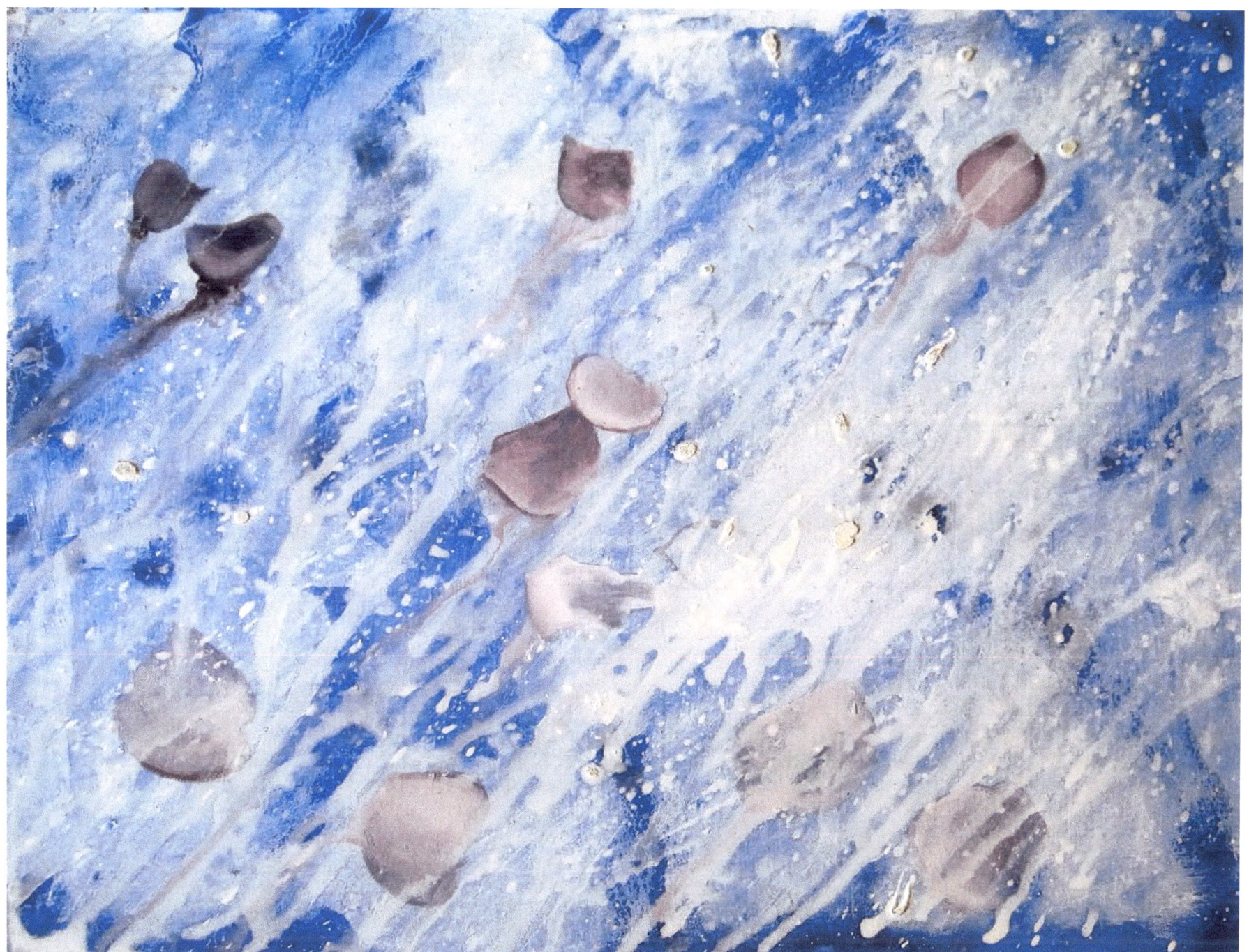

Taking a nap
feet planted
against a cool wall.

-Basho

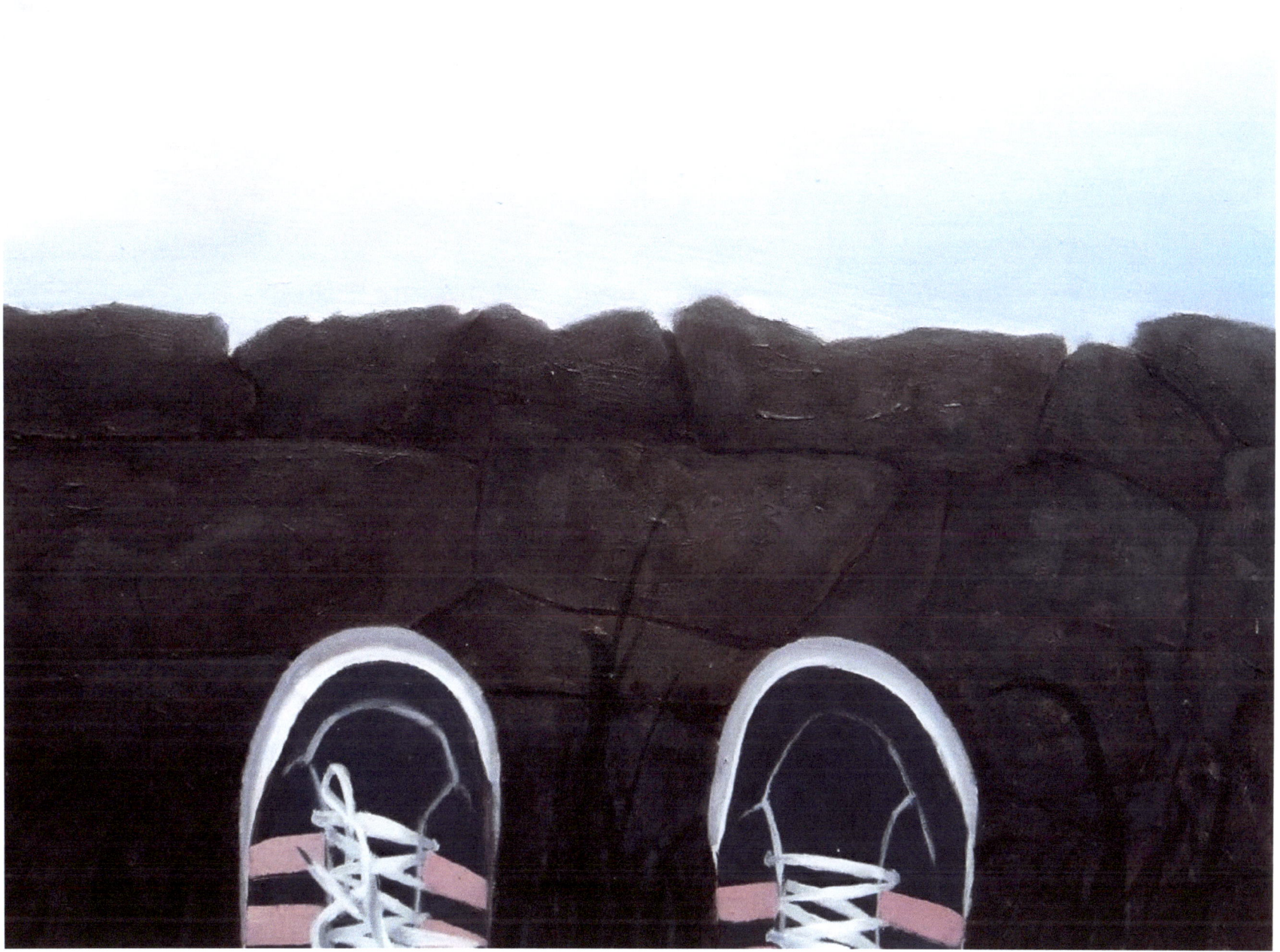

Blow if you will
fall wind – the flowers
have all faded.

-Gansan

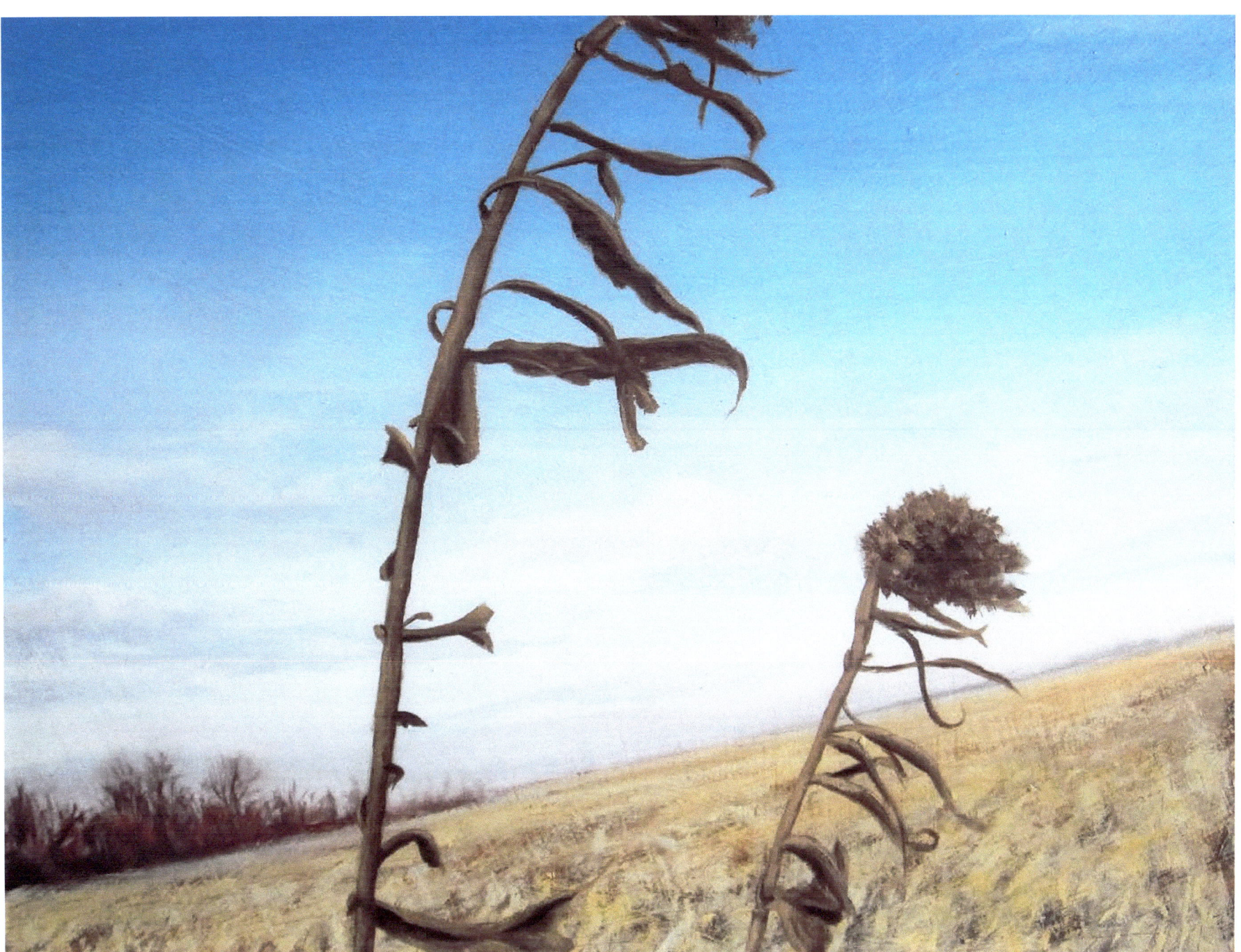

Leaves never fall
in vain- from all around
bells tolling.

- Chori

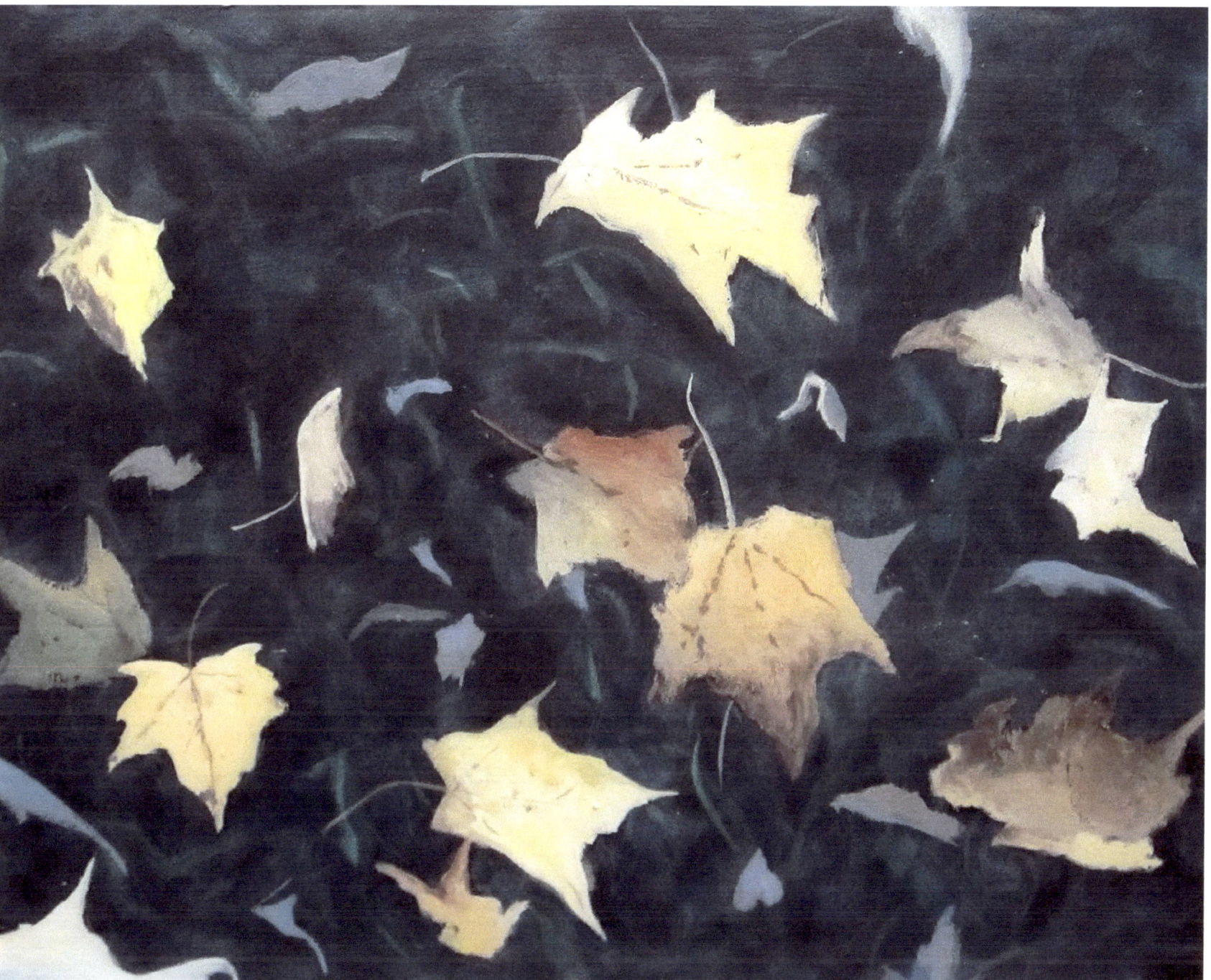

Autumn evening
there's joy also
in loneliness.

- Buson

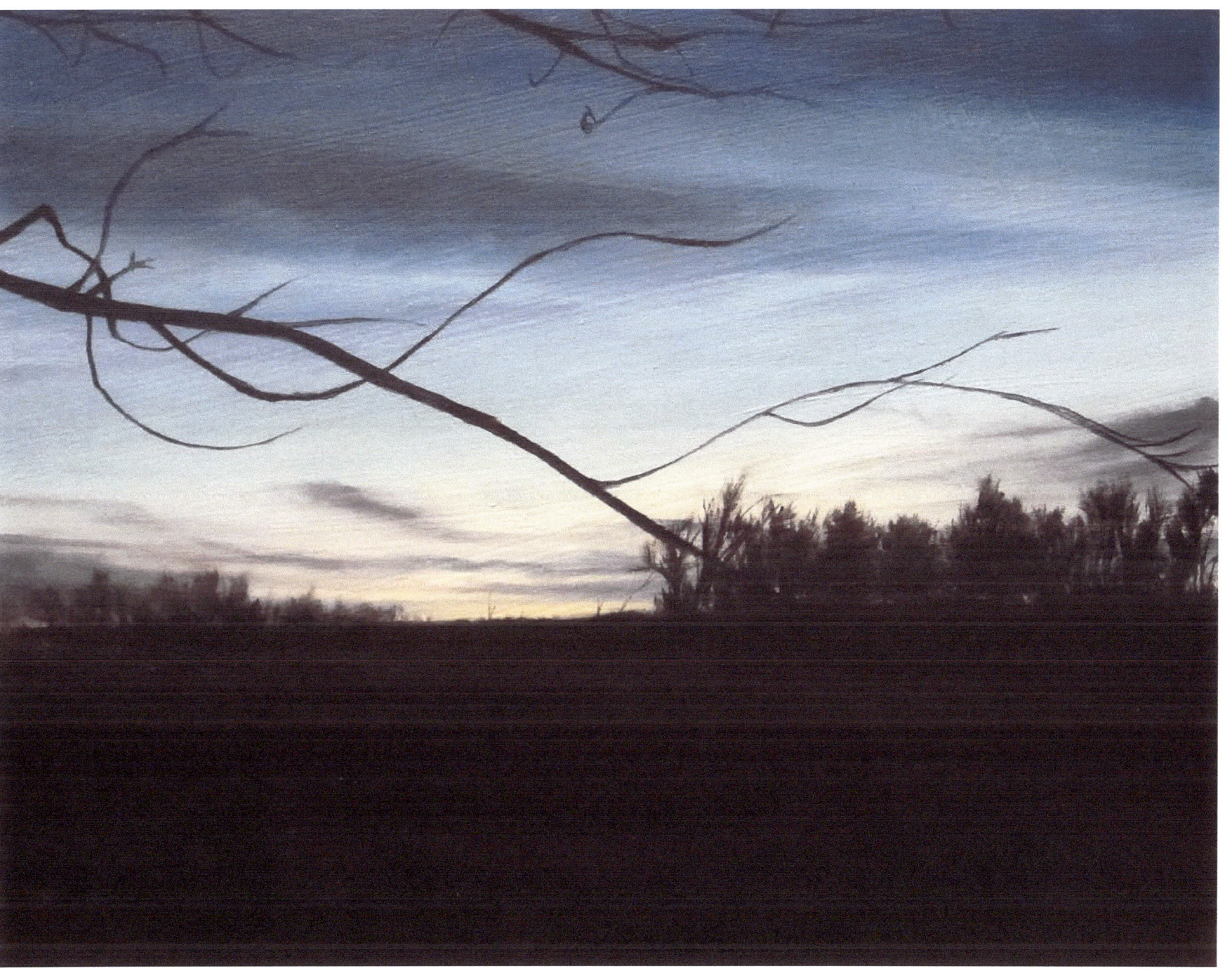

The clouds
are giving these moon watchers
a little break.

- Basho

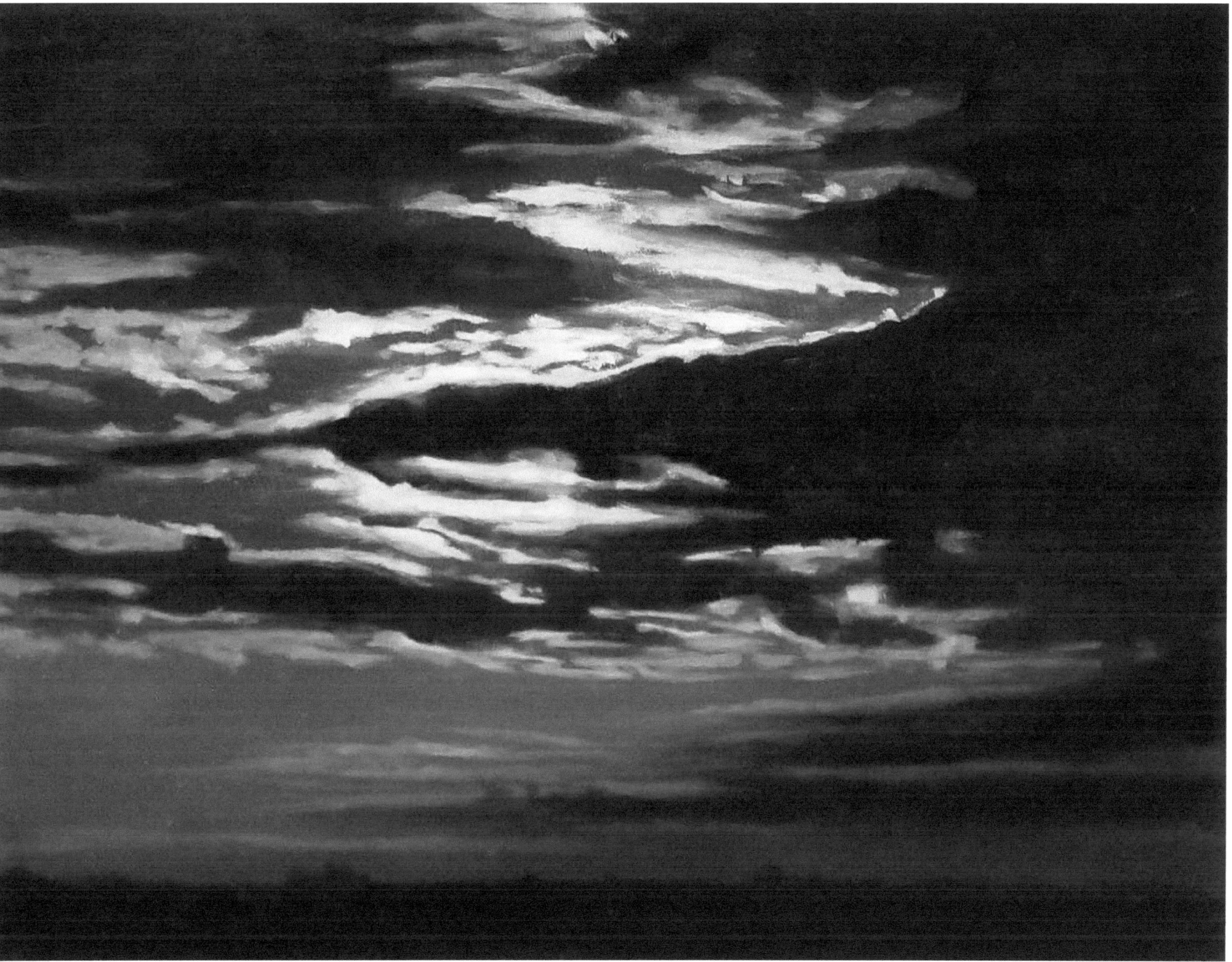

Midnight frost
I'd barrow
the scarecrow's shirt.

-Basho

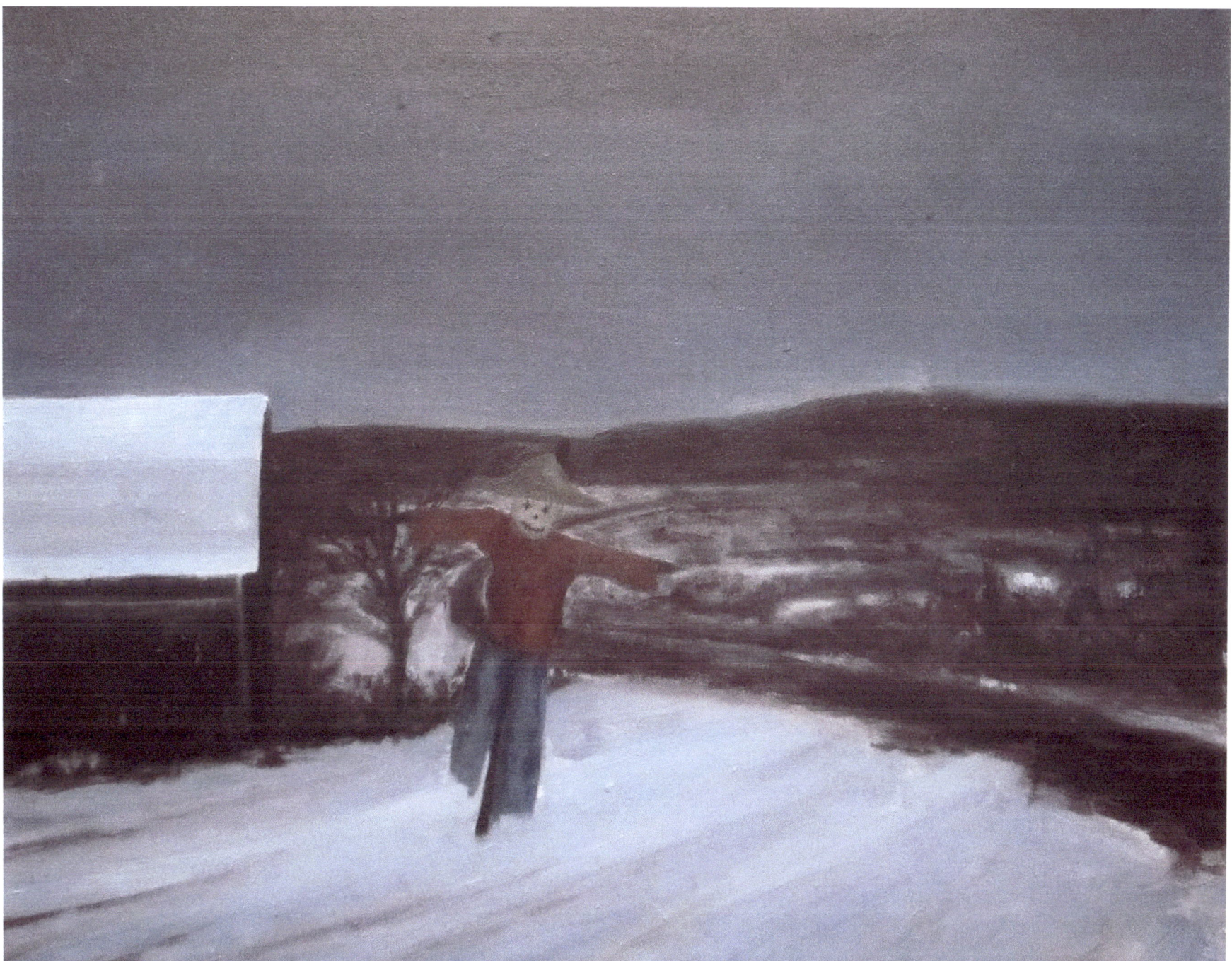

Winter solitude-
in a world of one color
the sound of wind.

-Basho

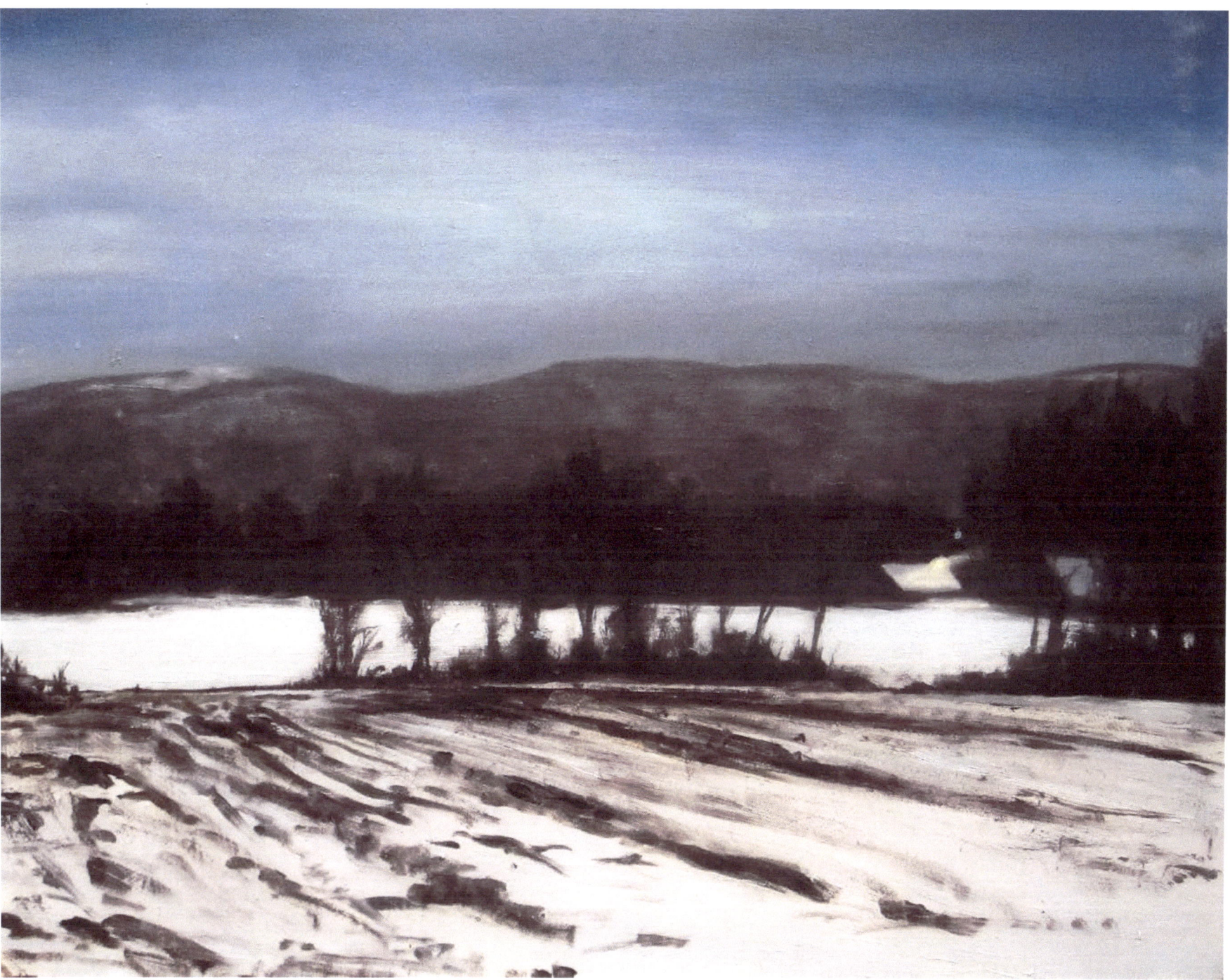

more books and art at: www.sky-in-session.com